Jesus said what now?

Jesus Said What Now?
The Most Mysterious Sayings and Doings of Jesus—Decoded

Copyright © 2023 David A. Holland

Book design by LynnCreative

ISBN 979-8-9885500-2-0 (print)
ISBN 979-8-9885500-0-6 (eBook)

DavidAHolland.com

DAVID A. HOLLAND

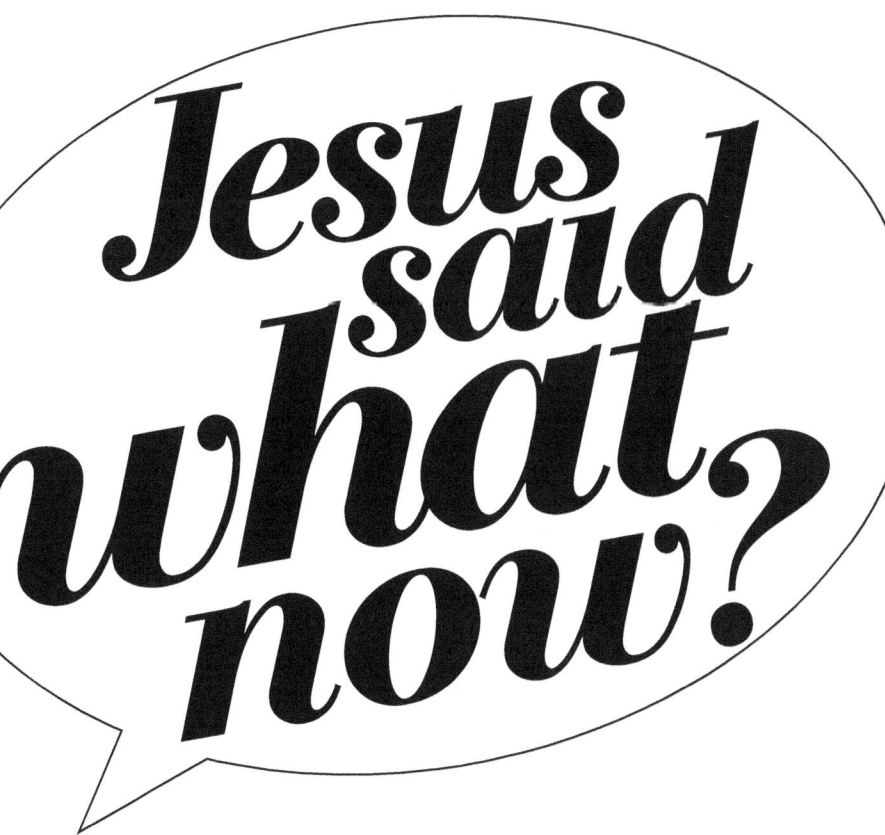

Jesus said what now?

*The most mysterious sayings and doings of Jesus—**decoded!***

Contents

Introduction

*A*lright ... it's honesty time. Let's get real and transparent together for a moment. Ready? (deep breath) Sometimes the Bible can be confusing. I can testify that I typed that sentence and lightning didn't strike me, and the earth didn't open up and swallow me. You know why? Because it's true!

If we're being real ... not religious ... real ... we can all admit that, from time to time, we read a verse or a passage in the Bible and say, "Wait ... what?" Or ... "What was THAT?" That is even true with the "red letters" in our Bibles. If you do most of your Bible reading online, you may not know about red letter Bibles where all the words of Jesus are in red type.

But yes, even some of the sayings (and doings) of Jesus are mysterious and, when we read them, leave us scratching our heads. Those "red letters" contain a lot of surprises. A few shocks. Even some scandals!

If you can relate, I have great news for you. I've chosen ten of the biggest, toughest mysteries and hard sayings and doings of Jesus and solved them for you. What you're about to discover is that often a little historical perspective, or the slight shift in theological paradigm, can take something that seemed confusing or contradictory (or just plain weird) and make it make beautiful sense. I've divided these mysteries into two categories: "Mysterious Doings" and "Mysterious Sayings."

Just ahead ... Mysteries solved! Hard sayings explained! Strange actions illuminated! Understanding enhanced! Faith strengthened! Let's go!

PART ONE

Mysterious Doings

Mysterious Doing #1

What did Jesus draw in the dust that terrified the men ready to stone the 'woman caught in adultery'?

*B*race yourself. I'm about to reveal the likely solution to a two-thousand-year-old mystery. One that has sparked curiosity and head scratching and speculation among Bible readers for two millennia.

If you're above a certain age, you might remember a show called "Unsolved Mysteries" from back in the nineties. If that's too old school for you, maybe you're more familiar with a recent series hosted by Lawrence Fishburne (Morpheus!) called "History's

Greatest Mysteries." Well, there's one historic mystery that has puzzled and vexed Christians through the ages. Let's begin with what the Bible itself tells us. We find it in the book of John:

> *Jesus returned to the Mount of Olives, but*
> *early the next morning he was back again*
> *at the Temple. A crowd soon gathered,*
> *and he sat down and taught them. As he*
> *was speaking, the teachers of religious law*
> *and the Pharisees brought a woman who*
> *had been caught in the act of adultery.*
> *They put her in front of the crowd.*
>
> *"Teacher," they said to Jesus, "this woman*
> *was caught in the act of adultery. The law of*
> *Moses says to stone her. What do you say?"*
>
> *They were trying to trap him into saying*
> *something they could use against him, but*
> *Jesus stooped down and wrote in the dust*
> *with his finger. They kept demanding an*

*answer, so he stood up again and said,
"All right, but let the one who has never
sinned throw the first stone!" Then he
stooped down again and wrote in the dust.*

*When the accusers heard this, they
slipped away one by one, beginning with
the oldest, until only Jesus was left in the
middle of the crowd with the woman.
Then Jesus stood up again and said to
the woman, "Where are your accusers?
Didn't even one of them condemn you?"*

"No, Lord," she said.

*And Jesus said, "Neither do I.
Go and sin no more."*
(John 8:1–11 NLT)

So, what could Jesus have possibly been writing in the dust?

Whatever it was—coupled with the simple stipulation, "Let the one who is without sin throw the first stone"—caused the assembled mob to, one-by-one, drop their stones and slink away.

Now, some Greek-language brainiacs have suggested that what Jesus actually said was, "Let the one who is without THIS sin, (i.e., the sin of adultery) cast the first stone." What I'm about to show you makes this interpretation a distinct possibility. But first, let's set the stage.

For some reason, because Jesus was writing in the dirt or dust, I always pictured this event happening outside on some dirt street or courtyard in a Judean village. After all, where else can a guy kneel down and start drawing in dust? But the first verse of this passage destroys that assumption.

Jesus was in the Temple, almost certainly at His favorite spot in the Temple courtyard to teach. That was a place called Solomon's Portico, a long colonnade or shaded porch supported by rows of marble columns. The floor of this space was smooth stone ... possibly limestone or marble. So where did the dust come from? It came from the feet of thousands upon thousands of visitors to the temple complex each day. Feet that had walked through the dusty, crowded streets of Jerusalem and up the hill to get there. There was almost certainly a thin layer of dust on those smooth stone floors at all times, providing the perfect "whiteboard" for Jesus to write upon.

But the location of Solomon's Portico for this incident prompts another question? Where did the mob get the stones they picked up in eager anticipation of getting to personally participate in the execution of a law-violating woman? Surely there weren't random stones laying around the ornate temple complex, right?

Random stones? No. But Jewish history reveals that there should have been a pile of stones lying conveniently nearby.

According to ancient Jewish literature, not quite 200 years earlier, one of the remnants of Alexander the Great's Greek empire got control of the Holy Land. Then in 156 BC, the current Greek ruler, Antiochus Epiphanes, ordered that a statue of Zeus be erected in the Temple's holy inner court and that a pig be sacrificed on the sacred altar there. The High Priest at the time refused to do so and was murdered right there in the Holy Place. Then one of the Greek soldiers did what the High Priest had refused to do, defiling the stone altar with pig's blood.

This prompted a successful Jewish revolt against the Greeks. And when the Jews regained control of the Temple, they broke the defiled altar apart, creating a pile of holy yet desecrated stones. Holy because this altar had been consecrated for the holiest place and purpose imaginable. Yet defiled because of the pig's blood.

That created a massive conundrum for the priesthood of Israel.

Those stones were too sacred to throw away but too defiled to be allowed to remain inside the main courts of the Temple. What to do?!

No one knew. So, they "temporarily" stacked the stones in a pile in the outer courts while the leaders tried to solve the puzzle of what to do with them. On the day we're examining, nearly two hundred years had passed, and that conundrum remained unresolved. So as Jesus regularly taught in Solomon's Portico, they were still there! THAT is almost certainly the source of the stones the mob picked up that day.

This brings us to what prompted them to put the stones down and slink away. I believe the answer lies in Numbers 5, where we find something that has come to be called the "Ordeal of the Bitter Water."

There, in the middle of a bunch of Levitical rules and regulations for the Israelite nation about to enter the Promised Land, we find a (frankly) bizarre instruction concerning what to do when a husband suspects his wife has been unfaithful. And before you ask, no, there was no process or recourse for a wife who suspected her husband of cheating. Keep in mind, we're talking about an era in world history in which women, even wives, were universally treated like either children or livestock. Once Jesus came and established a New Covenant based on better promises and sealed with His own blood, all of that began to change. But more on that in a moment. Back to the "Ordeal of Bitter Water."

If you doubt me, go read Numbers 5:11–31. I'll wait here.

Otherwise, take me at my word that in this passage we discover that if a husband thinks his wife has committed adultery, he is to bring her before a Levitical priest. And the priest is to take some consecrated water from the sacred bronze washbasin near the altar of sacrifice in the temple. (Yes, that same altar that provided the stones for the mob). He was to take some of that water and put it in a cup. Then he was to take some of the dust from the floor of the tabernacle and mix it into that water … and then speak a curse over that dirty water. The woman was to drink it. If she was innocent … it would not harm her. But if she was guilty … then she would become painfully ill, her belly would swell, and her womb would shrivel. She would be rendered barren.

Keep in mind, the gangs that threw this humiliated and terrified woman at Jesus' feet were Pharisees and scribes; that is, expert scholars of the law of Moses. They had been parsing the words of Exodus, Numbers, and Deuteronomy all their lives. Indeed, they would have almost certainly memorized them.

So when Jesus knelt and began drawing in the dust from the floor of the Temple complex, the symbolism would likely have been immediately recognizable to these men. Perhaps Jesus made it even clearer by drawing the outline of a cup in His "whiteboard." Or maybe he wrote something that pointed to that passage in Numbers. Even without it, they would have instantly thought of the "Ordeal of Bitter Water." They would have also assumed, initially, that Jesus was about to suggest this woman be subjected to this ordeal. They would have likely supported this because they were sure she was guilty. After all, the passage in John says she'd been caught *in the act*. On top of that, Jesus' final exhortation to the woman was, "Go and sin no more." But Jesus exploded their expectation by looking at her accusers and saying, "Let him who is without sin ... or maybe even ... without THIS sin ... cast the first stone." And then went back to drawing in the Temple dust. Can't you see Him taking a pinch of it between his fingers and sprinkling it as if into an invisible cup?

Do you see it? Jesus was saying, "Okay, guys. Let's have a priest mix up a Big Gulp-sized cup of floor-dust water, and we'll ALL have a drink. Let's let the Ordeal of Bitter Water decide who's pure enough to bash this woman's head in with a rock the size of a grapefruit."

John tells us that the oldest accusers were the first to drop their stones and walk away. Age does tend to bring wisdom. Age also means you've had a longer period of time to secretly sin.

Eventually, the lights came on for even the younger "scholars." It seems none of them wanted to take the "purity test" themselves.

So, what these "teachers of the religious law" designed as a trap for Jesus became a trap for themselves ... outing them as hypocrites.

There are so many powerful truths we can take away from this amazing incident. Of course, we see the kindness and compassion of our Savior. The impulse of the only one in that gathering who actually WAS without sin was to forgive and restore rather than execute judgment.

Going deeper, and knowing the rest of Jesus' story, we can understand that Jesus knew she didn't need to bear the penalty for her sins because Jesus was about to bear it Himself. Remember, this incident appears in John 8. By chapter nineteen, He'll be hanging on a cross, bearing the full weight of the guilt and shame of ALL humanity. Not just the sins of this nameless woman, but yours and mine as well.

There you have it. One of "History's Greatest Mysteries" ... solved. But what should you and I take away from this remarkable incident? Well, for one thing, we're all in desperate need of a Savior. All of us have sinned and fallen far, far short of God's standard of righteousness. It is only in accepting God's free gifts of mercy, forgiveness, and wholeness in Jesus that we have the privilege of being reconnected to Him and His Life. But when we do ... well, we get cleansed and wrapped in Jesus' perfect purity. We are clothed in

His own righteousness; that is, His own right-standing with God. Ephesians 2:8–9 in The Passion Translation reminds us:

> *For by grace you have been saved by faith.*
> *Nothing you did could ever earn this*
> *salvation, for it was the love gift from God*
> *that brought us to Christ! So no one will*
> *ever be able to boast, for salvation is never*
> *a reward for good works or human striving.*

That means pride and judgmentalism and finger-pointing have no place in the life of a person who has accepted such an extraordinary gift. Let's put down the stones and walk away.

Mysterious Doing #2

Why was Jesus so angered by the money changers and merchants in the Temple courtyard that He fashioned a whip and flipped over tables?

*H*ey friend, a big piece of a biblical puzzle is about to fall into place for you. Ready?

The "Jesus" revealed in the Gospels is generally gentle and kind ... kind to strangers, kind to children, patient with sinners, the teller of stories about birds and flowers and lost sheep and prodigal sons. That's the Jesus we see so consistently throughout Matthew, Mark, Luke, and John.

Which means most of us don't know what to do with the angry, violent Jesus of Mark 11. You know, the Jesus who fashioned a whip out of leather straps and went on a table-flipping rampage through the outer court of the Temple around the time of Passover. What was that about? Well, there is an answer to that question that may surprise you. And it's not what most of us have been taught. Or at least there is a big missing piece of the puzzle.

The account of Jesus "cleansing the Temple" is recorded in all four gospels. You can't say that about many of the events in Jesus' ministry. So, it must be pretty important. Let's examine Mark's account of the incident—which occurred in the opening days of the Passover week—verse by verse.

First a little context. Jesus has just had His "Palm Sunday Triumphal Entry" into Jerusalem where He fulfilled prophecy by entering the city gates on the back of a donkey and throngs of people hailed Him as the Messiah. Then:

And Jesus entered Jerusalem and came into
the temple area; and after looking around at
everything, He left for Bethany with the twelve,
since it was already late. (Mark 11:11 NASB)

Okay, this is very interesting. It's late in the day.
Jesus walks into the Temple complex. Mark said He
was "looking around at everything." And then Jesus
heads back out of the city to spend the night in
Bethany. Got it? Then He returns the next morning
with the disciples. So let's pick up the story in verse 15:

So they came to Jerusalem. Then Jesus went
into the temple and began to drive out those
who bought and sold in the temple, and
overturned the tables of the money changers
and the seats of those who sold doves. And
He would not allow anyone to carry wares
through the temple. Then He taught, saying
to them, "Is it not written, 'My house shall be
called a house of prayer for all nations'? But
you have made it a 'den of thieves.'" (NKJV)

Okay, let's establish a little more context here. According to the book of John, Jesus attended the Passover festival observances in all three years of His ministry. And Matthew, Mark, and Luke all make it clear that this particular Passover is His final one—the one that will lead to His arrest, trial, and crucifixion.

So, if this is His third Passover in Jerusalem since launching his ministry, why not get upset about the money changers on any of those previous visits to the Temple? Or any of the other times He'd visited the Temple during the great feasts and festivals? We're about to find out! The key to solving the mystery is in what Jesus Himself said in explanation of His violent actions.

But first, you need to understand the role of merchants and money changers at the Temple during the major feasts.

For centuries, Jews had been scattered across the Near East and around the vast Mediterranean Sea.

Many Jewish pilgrims traveled hundreds of miles to attend the spring and fall festivals. And it was impractical to try to bring animals for sacrifice and offering on those long journeys. You try dragging some sheep, goats, or birds to Jerusalem from Spain, North Africa, or Persia using First Century modes of travel. Not really an option. So Temple officials arranged for festival pilgrims to be able to purchase animals once they arrived. Thus, the merchants selling doves, goats, and other items near the Temple Mount. But there was another issue.

Citizens of the vast Roman Empire carried Roman coins. And as Jesus pointed out to a group of questioners one day, Roman coins carried an engraved image of the Roman Emperor, who was worshipped by Gentiles as a demigod throughout the empire. The Jewish leaders of that day had determined that it was a violation of the Second Commandment (no graven images) to use Roman coins to buy animals to be sacrificed in the heart of the Temple complex. So, they created a solution for this problem as well. They allowed currency exchange booths to be set up near the animal vendors so people could make their animal purchases in shekels. This is how both merchants (animal sellers) and money changers became a part of the Temple Mount scene whenever there was a major observance like Passover. Are you tracking?

Secondly, you need to understand the layout of Herod's Temple.

The Temple Jesus knew and visited frequently contained four separate "courts" ... arranged from outermost to innermost. Entering the Temple's outermost gate put you in the Court of the Gentiles, the only place on the holy hill that Gentiles could set foot. One step closer to the holy heart of the Temple complex was the Court of the Women, where ceremonially clean Jewish women were allowed to gather. This is as close as any Jewish woman was allowed to get to the Holy of Holies where God's presence was said to dwell. One layer deeper into the complex brought you to the Court of Israel (also called the Court of Men). Here, ceremonially clean Jewish men could stand just outside an even deeper level—the Court of Priests where the Levites carried out their sacred duties.

Here's the relevant question: Why have a "Court of the Gentiles" at a Jewish Temple? They built one because throughout the Old Testament period and throughout God's dealings with Israel, God had made it clear that He wanted to bless and reach the Gentiles through His relationship with Israel.

From the very beginning, when God told Abram that He was going to make him a great nation, He mentioned that through his seed "all the nations of the earth would be blessed." Note that term "the nations." Every time you see it in the Bible, it's referring to the Gentile peoples throughout the earth. Through numerous directives, prophecies, and psalms, God made it clear that part of Israel's role in the earth was to be a light to the Gentiles. THAT'S why there was a "Court of the Gentiles" on the Temple Mount. God wanted "God-fearing" Gentiles to be able to draw near to pray ... as a small down payment on the day the Messiah would come and make a way for both Jews and Gentiles to have direct access to His presence. Until that day, the Court of the Gentiles would serve as the one place on earth a Gentile could get close to the Presence of God and pray. BUT …

By Jesus' day, something had changed.

The Pharisees' power and influence had risen. And the Pharisees considered it defiling to even have to be in close proximity to a Gentile. They were considered lower than dogs. Several of Jesus' parables aimed at the Pharisees reference this revulsion. In the eyes of the Pharisees, the presence of Gentile pray-ers on God's holy hill was as offensive as having pigs or dogs roaming around on the Temple Mount. Having to walk past Gentiles to get to the Court of Men was just too much.

So, at some recent point, the Pharisees had successfully lobbied to have the currency exchange booths and sacrificial animal sellers moved farther up the hill to the Court of the Gentiles, effectively crowding the Gentiles out of their designated space.

It's possible they had even been banned from setting foot in the Temple complex altogether.

Adding to this violation of God's designated design, the money changers and the sellers apparently were corrupt and cheating the pilgrims. The former were offering sketchy exchange rates. The latter were over-charging the poor for the doves the law required them to purchase if they could not afford a lamb or a goat.

Armed with all that architectural and cultural context, let's return to Mark's narrative of Jesus' table-flipping spree. There is a detail in verse 11 that I've never heard anyone mention when preaching or teaching on this passage. Let's look at it again:

> *And Jesus entered Jerusalem and came into the temple area; AND AFTER LOOKING AROUND AT EVERYTHING, He left for Bethany with the twelve, since it was already late.* (Mark 11:11 NASB, emphasis added)

Jesus' actions when He returned the next day were not some impulsive, emotional, spur-of-the-moment reaction. Jesus was not suddenly triggered by what He saw there and just … snapped. No, Jesus had inspected the Temple complex the previous evening and, because it was late in the day, with the merchants and money changers likely packing up before sunset, Jesus left and returned to Mary and Martha's place in Bethany.

What Jesus did the next morning was calculated and fully authorized by His heavenly Father. Remember, Jesus once said that I only do those things that I see my heavenly Father doing. John's account adds the detail that Jesus took the time, probably that night, to fashion and weave together a multi-thonged whip out of leather strips. That was no quick process. Cutting and weaving a cat of nine tails out of leather gives a man time to think. And pray. And plan.

That next morning, He walked back into the Temple complex, whip in hand, and proceeded to do what we've all read and heard about many times. But why? My socialist friends love this passage because Jesus seems to be making an anti-capitalist statement by attacking both merchants and bankers. But is that the real take away here?

The answer lies in Jesus' statement of explanation. After arriving at the Court of the Gentiles and again finding it NOT filled with God-fearing Gentiles seeking to pray as close as possible to the Presence of God, but rather finding it filled with corrupt merchants cheating the poor and predatory money converters, Jesus drove them all out of the square and then, when challenged about it by the authorities, asked this question:

> *"Is it not written, 'My house shall be called*
> *A HOUSE OF PRAYER FOR ALL NATIONS?'*
> *But you have made it a 'den of thieves.'"*
> (Mark 11:17, NKJV emphasis added)

Jesus basically asked them if they'd read Isaiah 56:6–7, which in the NIV says:

*"And **foreigners** who bind themselves to
the Lord to minister to him, to love the name of
the Lord, and to be his servants, all who keep
the Sabbath without desecrating it and who
hold fast to my covenant—**these I will bring
to my holy mountain and give them joy in
my house of prayer.** Their burnt offerings
and sacrifices will be accepted on my altar;
**for my house will be called a house of
prayer for all nations.**"* (emphasis added)

Of course, the leaders and Pharisees had *read* it.
They just didn't *like* it. But Jesus knew what they did
not: He was only days away from laying Himself down
on a cross in order to make it possible for Jews and
people of every nation, tribe, color, and tongue to
have direct access to His heavenly Father. That He
was about to endure unspeakable suffering to provide
that access. That as He would cry out from the cross,
"It is Finished," the thick veil that symbolically separated all humans (except the High Priest) from the

Presence of their Father Creator would be torn completely in half.

What's the takeaway for you and me here?

Well, first, Jesus' intensity at this moment shouldn't be a surprise. He knew what we now know. That the "God who so loved the world" always intended to include the Gentiles in His plan of redemption. And excluding them from access for the sake of accommodating swindlers and hucksters was deeply, deeply offensive. The Pharisees and the religious leaders running the Temple were guilty of losing sight of the plot of why He had created the Jewish people. And in both action and words, Jesus delivered an indictment that said so in unmistakable terms.

So, let's keep God's white-hot love for lost mankind always in mind. God loves people. And in the form of God the Son became one of us to seek and save that which was lost. He's passionate about that. Let's share His passion.

Mysterious Doing #3

Jesus kills a defenseless tree.

We all have a favorite Jesus. We know and love Jesus: the welcomer of children.

We adore the Jesus: who "healed them all."

We reverence the Jesus: who weeps with compassion for the shepherdless sheep of the city of Jerusalem.

Me too! But what about Jesus: the fig tree killer? What do we do with Him?

If you're relatively new to the Bible, and you've read the account in Matthew 21 or Mark 11 where a hungry Jesus stops, gets upset at a fig tree for not having fruit on it, curses it, and then it dies ... well, you can be excused if you came away confused and wondering *Okay, What was THAT about?*

Another odd thing about this story is that it appears right in the middle of some really big, really momentous events. We're in the final week of Jesus' life before the cross. Just the day before Jesus had ridden into Jerusalem to throngs of adoring Israelites hailing Him as the promised Messiah. And right after this tree-killing incident, as we examined in the previous section, Jesus will shock and infuriate the caretakers of the sacred Temple by turning the outer court upside down in a wild outburst of righteous indignation. And He'll follow up that huge incident by issuing a series of stinging prophetic rebukes against the Pharisees and the religious leaders of Israel that will prove to be the final straw. Those condemnations will set in motion the chain of events that will end in His crucifixion. Within a week, He would be hanging from a cross for the sins of the world outside the walls of this very city. And He knew it.

But right in the middle of all this activity with clear, literally earth-shaking implications, we find this run in with ... a tree. A tree! It looked a little something like this:

> *On the following day, when they came from Bethany, he was hungry. And seeing in the distance a fig tree in leaf, he went to see if he could find anything on it. When he came to it, he found nothing but leaves, for it was not the season for figs. And he said to it, "May no one ever eat fruit from you again." And his disciples heard it."* (Mark 11:12–14 ESV)

A few verses later we read:

> *As they passed by in the morning, they saw the fig tree withered away to its roots. And Peter remembered and said to him, "Rabbi, look! The fig tree that you cursed has withered." And Jesus answered them, "Have faith in God."* (Mark 11:20–22 ESV)

Was that low blood sugar? I mean, it *did* say He was hungry. Why would Jesus, in the most momentous, pressure-packed, prophetically significant week of His life stop to curse a fig tree? And why would God make sure it got recorded in the gospel accounts of these world-changing final days of Jesus' ministry?

Well, here's your answer.

It is precisely BECAUSE these days were prophetically significant that Jesus made this unusual move.

Keep in mind, Jesus had spent the previous three years operating as the final prophet-messenger to the nation of Israel. He'd repeatedly warned of a coming judgment. Thundering like an Old Testament prophet, He'd pronounced "Woes" upon whole cities and entire strata of the Israelite society. He'd stood on a hilltop overlooking Jerusalem and wept because He knew what was coming to the city and the nation. In fact, a couple of chapters later, Jesus will be prophesying to His stunned disciples that something so cataclysmic was coming to Jerusalem that, when it was over, not one stone of the Temple would be left upon another.

This encounter with the tree makes perfect sense in this context once you know two things. One, the fig tree had long been a prophetic emblem of the nation of Israel. And two, fig trees leaf out and bear fruit at the same time. In other words, a fig tree with leaves is publicly advertising itself as being fruitful.

The account in Mark lets us know that Jesus noticed this tree had leaves on it, even though it was not the proper season for fig trees to sprout leaves and bear fruit. When Jesus approached it, He saw that the tree was guilty of false advertising. It was, in essence, *a hypocrite*. It was claiming to have fruit yet had none. It was barren.

Jesus, in His office as a prophet, had repeatedly denounced the hypocrisy of the Pharisees and the other elite Jewish leaders of that day. For example, three separate times in Matthew 23, Jesus shouts: "Woe to you, scribes and Pharisees, hypocrites!"

Are you getting the idea that Jesus is not cool with this whole hypocrisy thing?

The third and final "woe" went something like this:

> *"Woe to you, scribes and Pharisees, hypocrites! For you are like whitewashed tombs, which **outwardly** appear beautiful, but within are full of dead people's bones and all uncleanness. So you also **outwardly** appear righteous to others, but **within you are full of hypocrisy** and lawlessness.* (Matthew 23:27–28 ESV, emphasis added)

Do you see it? This tree was a living parable for the nation and her leaders! Well, not a *living* parable. More of a DYING parable. Jesus was signifying that unless the hypocrites repented of their hypocrisy, and quickly, they and the city would eventually suffer the same fate as the tree: dying under a curse. The old covenant of Moses with its 613 Levitical laws had served its purpose. It had kept the Jewish nation intact long enough to get the promised Messiah into the earth. But now, it was about to become "obsolete" and begin "passing away." (See: Hebrews 8:13)

In a few days, Jesus would shed His blood and become High Priest and sacrificial Lamb of a new covenant based on better promises. And forty years later, almost to the day, the armies that would eventually reduce the Temple to rubble would surround Jerusalem.

THAT is why, in the critical final week of His ministry to Israel, Jesus stopped to rebuke a hypocritical tree. Not so crazy after all, it seems.

So what are the takeaways for you and me here?

Well, it's fairly obvious that God values authenticity in our faith ... as opposed to pretense and putting on a good show. We can be honest before God and transparent before others. Yes, we're flawed, frail, fragile, and prone to mistakes. Yet we're loved anyway. In Christ, we're righteous and approved and accepted. And our fruitfulness as trees of God is not a result of our self-discipline, fleshly effort, willpower, or talent. No; if we're fruitful, it's solely because we're connected to Jesus ... the true Vine. Apart from Him, we can do nothing.

Let's be authentic.

Having solved three of Jesus' most perplexing *doings*, let's now spend the balance of our time together unraveling some of the most misunderstood and bewildering things He *said*.

PART TWO

Mysterious Sayings

Mysterious Saying #1

Pluck out my eye? Cut off my hand? Really, Jesus?

I've never been extremely athletic, but there was a time, back in my college years, where I was an exceptional ping-pong player. Table tennis, to use the fancier term, doesn't so much require raw athleticism as it does hand-eye coordination. Would you like to know what compromises hand-eye coordination?

Hacking off your hands and poking out your eyes. It's true!

As I scandalously mentioned in the "Introduction," the Bible can be confusing sometimes. There, I said it again. You can cancel me, but it's true. Sorry, not sorry. The Bible can be confusing and can sometimes "seem" to contradict itself ... especially if you pick it up and start reading it like it fell out of the sky three weeks ago. Or if you try to read it like a college textbook where you assume all the information has been thoughtfully organized in a logical sequence. That's not your Bible. Don't get me wrong. The Bible is a miracle. It's powerful. Every word is God-breathed. But occasionally ... unless you know what you're looking at ... without some context and a proper grid ... it will seem sometimes to contradict itself.

Let me give you a perfect example. If you read Paul's letters, and books in your New Testament like Romans, Galatians, Ephesians, Philippians, and Colossians, you'll discover a wonderful, liberating, "good news" truth. You'll discover grace. You'll start to absorb the astonishing good news that your connection to God isn't about your performance, your good works, or your righteousness. The "good news" of the New Covenant is that accepting God's free gift of salvation puts you "in Christ" ... "in Jesus" ... and that means your connection to God is based on Jesus' performance, Jesus' good works, and Jesus' righteousness, not your own. That's actually better than *good* news. It's fantastic news!

As a frail, fallible, flawed work-in-progress, it's so liberating and comforting to read a Scripture like Romans 8:1, "Therefore there is now no condemnation at all for those who are in Christ Jesus" (ESV). Or 2 Corinthians 5:21, "God made Him who knew no sin to be sin for us, that we might become the righteousness of God in Him" (MEV). But here's the challenge:

Just about the time those amazing truths are about to get rooted into our sense of identity in God, we flip over to the Gospels, like to Matthew 5, and hear Jesus —Jesus Himself!—say something like, "If your right eye is causing you to sin, tear it out and throw it away! If your right hand is causing you to sin, cut it off and throw it away from you." And not only does Jesus say this in chapter five, but He repeats Himself again in chapter eighteen!

Whoa! Hold on! I thought … but … didn't Paul say …?

Yes. I know. Well, I have good news for you today. The Bible isn't contradicting itself. If we're confused, it's simply a sign we're not "rightly dividing" it. And I have even better news for you:

God doesn't expect you to start plucking out eyeballs and hacking off limbs.

You're about to understand why. Let's read that whole passage from Matthew 5. It, by the way, is part of Jesus' long "Sermon on the Mount" to a throng of Jewish people.

> *"Now if your right eye is causing you to sin, tear it out and throw it away from you; for it is better for you to lose one of the parts of your body, than for your whole body to be thrown into hell. And if your right hand is causing you to sin, cut it off and throw it away from you; for it is better for you to lose one of the parts of your body, than for your whole body to go into hell."* (Matthew 5:29–30 NASB)

Okay, that sounds VERY serious. Our Savior and King has just instructed a group of listeners to pluck out an eye or lop off a hand if either one is causing them to sin. And He suggested that committing a sin would send you to hell! Now, it's important to note that just prior to giving this instruction, Jesus had ALSO said that just looking at someone who is not your spouse with desire is a sin equivalent to committing adultery. So ... if we we're all to take this command literally, we'd all be walking around without either eyes or hands. And I bet you've noticed that most preachers and teachers still have both eyes and hands intact! (Unless they also regularly drink and operate farm machinery.)

As I mentioned, Jesus says pretty much the same thing in Matthew 18. In both sermons, Jesus is talking to people of the Old Covenant about the coming "kingdom" of heaven or kingdom of God. He's telling them it's near. At hand. Coming soon. Right around the corner. And He's encouraging them to be prepared. We now know that the soon-coming kingdom was the "New Covenant," which He would soon inaugurate through His sacrificial death, resurrection, and ascension to the throne of heaven.

So here's what you need to know about these puzzling words of Jesus and pretty much ALL the red letters in your red-letter Bible, by the way.

Jesus came to embody three Old Testament offices: prophet, priest, and king.

We're very familiar with the "king" part. Just before His ascension, He told His disciples that all authority in both heaven and earth had been given to Him. (Matthew 28:18) We know that He then took His seat on the throne at the right hand of the Father. (See: Romans 8:34 and about 50 other verses in your Bible.) Concerning the *King* part of the prophet-priest-king equation ... Check!

Many also know about the *Priest* part of that equation. The prayer Jesus prayed in John 18 is called the "high priestly prayer." And the book of Hebrews makes it clear that Jesus was operating in priest mode throughout the days leading up to and throughout His crucifixion. So ... Priest? Check!

But what about the "prophet" piece of that trifecta? Well, as I pointed out in the previous segment, Jesus actually spent most of His three-year ministry operating as the final prophetic voice to the people of the Old Covenant. For three years He traveled throughout Israel—north to south and back again, from the sea to the River Jordan and beyond—going through all Israel's villages, visiting all the synagogues. And everywhere He went, He declared the imminent coming of the Kingdom of God and called God's covenant people to repent.

But repent *to* what? To what standard or code of morals were Jesus' listeners to repent TO? There was only one standard in place at that time: the true spirit of the Levitical Law. The New Covenant and its new "law of love" did not yet exist. Jesus couldn't possibly have been calling Jewish people to repent to a standard that didn't exist. Nevertheless, at that very moment, all but a few in Israel had abandoned the true spirit of the Mosaic Law. Many had walked away from observance all together. Others, like the Pharisees and Sadducees, pretended to observe it, but Jesus was constantly pointing out their corruption and hypocrisy.

So, very much like an Old Testament prophet, Jesus was calling the Jewish people of that generation to repent under the old covenant so they would have soft hearts to receive the message of the new one when it came. And that new covenant with its new "law of love" could only come AFTER the cross. Just like an Old Testament prophet, Jesus consistently warned His hearers of a coming judgment for those who hardened their hearts. And judgment WAS coming. As I pointed out in a previous segment, forty years after Jesus' death and resurrection, Roman armies would surround Jerusalem. Hundreds of thousands of Jewish people would die. Hundreds of thousands of others would be carried off into slavery. Jerusalem and many of the surrounding cities of Israel would be reduced to smoldering rubble.

NOW you have some context to understand Jesus' messages about eyes and hands. In His role as the final Old Covenant prophet, Jesus was saying, "Hey! Repent and get right under the current covenant so you'll have ears to hear the good news about the new one when it's being preached after my death, resurrection, and ascension to the throne." Or put another way, Jesus was saying, "Don't harden your heart to God now because, on the other side of the cross, you're going to need a soft heart to say "yes" and enter the long-awaited kingdom of God and thereby miss the coming outpouring of judgment."

THAT, dear friend, is why Jesus would say to His Jewish hearers, "Respond in faith to my message of repentance NOW, because it will put you in a position to enter the kingdom when it arrives. This is so important that if your eye or hand is keeping you from responding in belief now, you'd be better off getting rid of them than end up facing the hellish judgment that is coming."

With all that in mind, let's look at Jesus' second mention of plucking out eyes in Matthew 18:6–8. The context here is that Jesus is talking about the coming kingdom and specifically condemning "stumbling blocks" who would keep Jewish people from embracing the message of the kingdom. He said:

> *"These little ones believe in me. It would be best for the person who causes one of them to lose faith to be drowned in the sea with a large stone hung around his neck. How horrible it will be for the world because it causes people to lose their faith. Situations that cause people to lose their faith will arise. How horrible it will be for the person who causes someone to lose his faith! If your hand or your foot causes you to lose your faith, cut it off and throw it away. It is better for you to enter life disabled or injured than to have two hands or two feet and be thrown into everlasting fire. If your eye causes you to lose your faith, tear it out and throw it away. It is better for you to enter life with one eye than to have two eyes and be thrown into hellfire."* (GW)

Now in both passages, Jesus talks about being thrown in the "hell." But the underlying Greek word here is not "hades." Jesus did use the word *hades* from time to time, such as when He was talking about the Church and said, "The gates of *hell* shall not prevail against it." But ... here Jesus used the word *Gehenna* ... a desecrated place of burning outside of Jerusalem that was synonymous with God's judgment. The hearers of Jesus' day would have known He was talking about a coming judgment against rebellion here.

This is great news for you and me.

It means Jesus and Paul are in full agreement. Jesus, the prophetic voice to that generation of Jews, desperately wanted as many of His fellow Jews as possible to escape the coming judgment and experience new life in the coming kingdom.

In that kingdom, Jesus would not only bear the weight and guilt of their sin, but He would also be their righteousness. He would be their complete satisfaction and fulfillment of everything the Law demanded.

What's your takeaway here? It's great news!

You can put the meat cleaver away!

You can keep your eyes and your hands, my friend. Jesus bore the judgment you and I deserved. If you're a born-again believer, He's declared you righteous.

That means your marching orders are in Romans 12:1. We're to present our whole bodies ... our whole being ... as a "living sacrifice." The operative word there is LIVING. You're now free to consecrate your hands, your eyes, your whole body to the service of the King who died for you, who clothed you in HIS righteousness, and irrevocably gifted you with eternal life.

Mysterious Saying #2

Sell everything you have.

*F*or centuries, there have been sincere people who believed that being a Christian required taking a vow of poverty. That owning anything was incompatible with following Jesus. Where would people get such an idea?

Ground zero for this belief is the passage we're going to explore for the next few minutes. It's a story found in Luke 18, with versions that also appear in Matthew 19 and Mark 10. I'm talking about the story of "the Rich Young Ruler."

We're examining the mysterious and "hard" sayings of Jesus. And what we're about to hear Jesus say in this passage is pretty hardcore! Let's begin with verse 18:

> *And a ruler asked him, "Good Teacher, what must I do to inherit eternal life?" And Jesus said to him, "Why do you call me good? No one is good except God alone. You know the commandments: 'Do not commit adultery, Do not murder, Do not steal, Do not bear false witness, Honor your father and mother.'" And he said, "All these I have kept from my youth."* (ESV)

Okay, let's pause here for a moment and take note of a couple of things. It's super interesting that when this man asked Jesus what he needed to do to inherit eternal life, Jesus pointed him to the ten commandments. To be specific, He cites *five* of the ten commandments. Jesus mentions the five "doing" commandments but doesn't mention the other five, which are more about the attitudes of the heart. Those include: don't worship other gods; keep the Sabbath; don't covet other people's stuff, etc.

We should also note that the initial answer Jesus gave was a direct reflection of how this young man framed his question. He asked, "Good teacher, what must I DO to inherit eternal life?"

The kid asked a "DO" question, so he got a "DO" answer.

And this hotshot was confident that he had done all the "DOs" ... since childhood! Somewhere along the lines, the scribes and Pharisees had studied the five books of Moses and determined that there were precisely 613 laws and regulations embedded in them. 613 dos and do nots! And like many of the Pharisees of Jesus' day, he was confident that he was successfully keeping ALL of them. Of course, Jesus used the entire "Sermon on the Mount" in Matthew 6 to show people like him they were wrong about that, but let's keep reading. We'll pick it back up at verse 22 ...

When Jesus heard this, he said to him, "One thing
you still lack. Sell all that you have and distribute
to the poor, and you will have treasure in heaven;
and come, follow me." But when he heard these
things, he became very sad, for he was extremely
rich. Jesus, seeing that he had become sad, said,
"How difficult it is for those who have wealth
to enter the kingdom of God! For it is easier for
a camel to go through the eye of a needle than
for a rich person to enter the kingdom of God."
Those who heard it said, "Then who can be
saved?" But he said, "What is impossible with
man is possible with God." (Luke 18:22–25 ESV)

Why did Jesus say this to this man?

Was Jesus really suggesting that
keeping the Ten Commandments
and getting rid of all your stuff
gets you a ticket to heaven?

It sure looks like it at first blush. If so, how can we possibly reconcile this with the hundreds of verses in the New Testament that make it clear that salvation is a grace gift from God that we receive by faith, not of works, and that even saving faith itself is a gift!? See Ephesians 2:8–9 or read Romans 10:13 which says, "For everyone who calls on the name of the Lord will be saved."

NOT … "Everyone who calls on the name of the Lord AND strictly obeys all the commandments AND gets rid of all their material possessions will be saved." Right? What about all our efforts at righteousness being nothing but filthy, smelly rags, as Isaiah revealed? What about Paul's declaration in Romans 3:20: "For by works of the law no human being will be justified in his sight …" (ESV). What's Jesus talking about here? This is quite a mystery!

Well, the key to solving this mystery is the same one that unlocks a lot of the other mysteries and "hard sayings" of Jesus that we're exploring in these pages. The key is understanding that in the majority of His preaching and teaching, Jesus is NOT laying out New Covenant truth; He's functioning as the final Old Testament prophet, calling the entire Israelite nation to repentance to the spirit of the Mosaic Law. Jesus knew that on the other side of the cross, when the New Covenant and the kingdom had come, such people would be the ones with soft hearts to hear the good news of the kingdom, based on a new and better covenant, and receive it.

THAT, my friend, is why Jesus asked this man to lay down his great wealth and follow Him. You may recall that on another occasion Jesus was asked what the greatest commandment was. His answer was to "... love the Lord your God with all your heart and with all your soul and with all your mind and with all your strength" (Mark 12:30).

Remember, this guy had just claimed to be keeping ALL the commandments. Jesus is essentially saying, "Okay, bro. Let's test that assertion." He presented this man with a test of his obedience to the greatest of all commandments: to love God more than you love anything else. So ... which did this guy love more? God or His wealth?

Jesus wasn't saying that ridding yourself of all earthly possessions and taking a vow of poverty was necessary to going to heaven.

He was exposing this dude as a fraud. A liar.

And by the way, lying violates the ninth commandment, so ... BUSTED again! Jesus was also saying that, for THIS man, coming into alignment with the greatest Old Covenant commandment would position his heart to say yes to God's offer of the free gift of salvation that would be extended only AFTER Jesus laid down on that cross and then walked out of that tomb!

Think about it. This guy could have become the 13th disciple. The Judas replacement! Imagine for a moment that he'd said yes to Jesus' challenge and offer. If so, like the rest of the disciples, he would not have received the eternal life he was seeking until AFTER the death and resurrection of Jesus. He could not. Only AFTER Jesus' sacrifice was the New Covenant and the kingdom it ushered in available.

Like the rest of the disciples, he would have been confused and powerless until the new birth and outpouring of the Holy Spirit on the Day of Pentecost.

So, what are the takeaways for you and me here?

God doesn't require a vow of poverty as a precondition for giving you eternal life. *Whoever calls upon the name of the Lord shall be saved.* But once we become His son or daughter, the most natural, most appropriate thing in the world is to hold everything we've been given with an open hand ... ready to give and share at any time. Not so that we can go to heaven. But simply in order to live in alignment with heaven's values. To live in alignment with who we already are in Christ.

God so loved that He *gave* ... John 3:16 tells us. And we're never more like our heavenly Father than when we're giving freely from a heart of love. As a believer, when you're living in alignment with who you really are, you have stuff, but your stuff doesn't have you. Your identity is not rooted in what you have. Your identity is wholly and completely rooted in WHOSE you ARE.

When that's the case, you're free! And when you're free, you're ready to give all, leave all, go anywhere, do anything ... not because this earns you salvation, but because you are already irrevocably His, and this is who you are, in Him!

Mysterious Saying #*3*

Wait. Did Jesus just call that pitiful lady a "dog"?

Why did Jesus repeatedly rebuff a pitiful, pleading woman with the demon-possessed daughter, going as far as to say that it was inappropriate to "give the children's bread to dogs?"

Here, we're about to tackle one of the hardest of the hard sayings of Jesus. Okay, let's be honest. It's one of those incidents in the Gospels that makes those of us who love Jesus and have experienced His extraordinary love and kindness ... uncomfortable. And maybe a little confused. I'm talking about the account we find in Matthew 15 of Jesus and the Gentile woman from Syrophoenicia; that's modern-day southern Lebanon.

For those of us who have experienced Jesus the Good Shepherd, Jesus the Redeemer, the gentle Jesus of the gospels who welcomed children to His lap, "healed all," and turned no one away, this incident stands out as shockingly uncharacteristic. It's stunning, really.

If you're not sure what I'm talking about, let's read it together:

> *Then Jesus left Galilee and went north to the region of Tyre and Sidon. A Gentile woman who lived there came to him, pleading, "Have mercy on me, O Lord, Son of David! For my daughter is possessed by a demon that torments her severely." But Jesus gave her no reply, not even a word.* (Matthew 15:21–23a NLT)

Awkward! Yes, you read that correctly. A Gentile woman approaches Jesus and pleads for her little girl to be released from demonic torment. And Jesus doesn't even acknowledge her request. He just keeps on walking like she's not there.

The desperate woman clearly persists in her pleading because the next thing we read is:

> *Then his disciples urged him to send her*
> *away. "Tell her to go away," they said.*
> *"She is bothering us with all her begging."*
> *Then Jesus said to the woman, "I was sent*
> *only to help God's lost sheep—the people*
> *of Israel." But she came and worshiped*
> *him, pleading again, "Lord, help me!" Jesus*
> *responded, "It isn't right to take food from*
> *the children and throw it to the dogs."*
> (vss. 23b–26 NLT, emphasis added)

Okay, now this awkward situation has escalated into outright horrifying for us Jesus fans. When Jesus finally speaks, He seems to refer to this desperate non-Jewish person as a "dog." That sounds like insult enough in our place and time, but in the Middle East, referring to someone as a dog was close to being the worst thing you could call someone.

What's going on here? You're about to find out, but first let's hear, "the rest of the story." After Jesus made the comment about giving the children's food to dogs, we pick up with verse 27:

> She replied, "That's true, Lord, but even dogs are allowed to eat the scraps that fall beneath their masters' table." "Dear woman," Jesus said to her, "your faith is great. Your request is granted."
> And her daughter was instantly healed. (NLT)

Whew! Now we're talking! *That's* the Jesus we expected to encounter.

So what turned Jesus around so quickly?

And more importantly, what explains His initial, indifferent, even callous response to a poor woman who clearly had tremendous faith in Jesus' power to deliver and save? Well, I'm about to bring a couple of things to your attention that, once you understand them, will snap this whole bewildering picture into sharp focus.

The first involves reminding you of something that has been a key in several of our previous mysteries. Namely, the understanding that Jesus spent his first three years in ministry operating as a *prophet* to that generation of Jews living in the land of promise. If Jesus' only mission assignment was to die on the cross, He could have had a two-week ministry. So, why a three-year ministry? Because there was another job to do … another role to play … before becoming the spotless Lamb who would take away the sins of the world. Jesus was prophesied to be, and anointed to serve as, a prophet.

Which is why Mark's gospel begins with Jesus taking the prophetic baton from John the Baptist. John had preached, "Repent for the kingdom of God is at hand." (See: Matthew 3:2) And as soon as John got taken offline, so to speak, by being thrown in a dungeon, it became Jesus' message, too. Here's Mark 1:14–15:

> *Now after John was arrested, Jesus came*
> *into Galilee, proclaiming the gospel of*
> *God, and saying, "The time is fulfilled,*
> *and the kingdom of God is at hand; repent*
> *and believe in the gospel."* (ESV)

Hey, that's John's sermon! That's also the language, the vocabulary, of a prophet. And that message wasn't just for the people of Galilee that week. Look at Matthew 9:35:

> *Jesus was going through ALL the*
> *cities and villages, teaching in their*
> *synagogues and proclaiming the gospel*
> *of the kingdom, and healing every*
> *disease and every sickness.* (NASB)

As we've seen previously, Jesus spent the next three years traversing the nation north and south, east and west, calling all Israelites to return to faithfulness to the true spirit of the Old Covenant. Why?

Because the kingdom was near in time.

And it seems that, somehow, repenting to the spirit ... not just the letter ... but the true *spirit* of the Old was key to having a soft heart to receive the New when it arrived on the other side of the cross. The New Covenant Jesus made possible was that "kingdom" He was talking about. And this prophetic message was for ALL Israelites: the hyper-observant Pharisees, the marginally observant fisherman and farmers, and those who had completely abandoned the faith.

Jesus knew the day of redemption for the Gentiles was coming soon, but only IF He successfully fulfilled His mission. But during His three-year prophetic ministry, Jesus was single-mindedly focused on the first vital phase of that mission. In Jesus' own words to the Syrophoenician woman, that mission was calling "the lost sheep of the house of Israel" to repentance and alerting them that a new day was about to dawn.

When Jesus told the woman, in essence, "I can't help you now; my focus is the lost sheep of the house of Israel," He wasn't lying. In that season, that *was* the mission. Of course, Jesus knew the cross was coming. In fact, in the very next chapter in Matthew we see Jesus saying making this plain:

> *From that time Jesus began to show his disciples that he must go to Jerusalem and suffer many things from the elders and chief priests and scribes, and be killed, and on the third day be raised.* (Matthew 16:21 ESV)

Here's what you need to understand about Jesus' thoughts and frame of mind in this encounter with this woman. If Jesus couldn't complete His prophetic mission and then move on to His High Priestly mission on the cross, there would be no hope for this woman's daughter. Or any Gentile woman, man, or child, for that matter. Ever.

It is no exaggeration to say the eternal fate of millions ... billions ... including this poor woman and her tormented daughter ... hung in the balance.

So THAT, my friend, is why He would tell a desperate Canaanite woman that NOW was not His time to help people like her. That time was coming. But before that could happen, He had to complete his first mission to "the lost sheep of the House of Israel." But upon completing it—on the other side of the cross, the resurrection, and His ascension to the throne at God's right hand—well then, the door not only to deliverance but also eternal life itself would be thrown open to that little girl and a whole world of people, present and future.

Even so, at the end of the day, that woman's *faith* overcame Jesus' *focus*.

Her single-minded persistence broke through Jesus' single-minded pursuit of His mission. As a result, she became perhaps the first Gentile on earth to receive a sneak preview of the coming king-dom Jesus had been preaching to His Jewish brothers and sisters. A kingdom where both Jews and Gentiles would sit side by side at the King's banquet table.

Oh, and what of that insulting reference to this woman being a "dog"? Wasn't that a bit ... excessive?

Well, it's not nearly as harsh as it might seem in our English translations. The Greek word for adult dog, as in a stray dog ... is *kuon*. But that's not the Greek word Jesus used. He used the word *kunarion* ... a word used to describe a small dog ... in other words, a puppy. He called her a pet puppy dog. (Awww!)

Although dogs were considered filthy and unclean and were never kept as pets in ancient Israel ... they *were* commonly kept as pets in the Greek and Roman culture from which this woman came.

Jesus clearly knew who He was talking to.

Which is why he used the imagery of tossing a pet puppy the food meant for the hungry children of the house. And why her clever reply about crumbs from the table resonated instantly with Jesus.

So, what are the takeaways for you and me here?

Well, first of all, we now know nothing in this story should cause us to question Jesus' compassion and kindness. He was a perfect, living, breathing representation of the Father's heart. A Father that so loved the world that He sent His only Son to restore us to Himself. Jesus was and still is, first and foremost, a redeemer.

Secondly, I get it. I'm a dad. My bride and I raised three amazing girls, and I can recall numerous occasions when they were little where I was focused, task-oriented, and in the middle of something important when one of them would start pulling on my pants leg with an urgent request. In those moments, my response was often not unlike that of Jesus, "Not now, little puppy. I'm in the middle of something very important here."

That response didn't mean I didn't care.

It didn't mean I didn't adore them. It simply meant that I was engaged in big things they couldn't possibly understand. Often things that would impact their long-term well-being. That's what we see in our Savior here.

So perhaps we can also take a lesson about priorities and mission from this story. Jesus understood His assignment from God. He understood that heavenly assignments have stages, steps, and seasons. And that timing matters.

Maybe you should be aware that you, too, have a mission or assignment from the Father. And there will always be distractions and seemingly good activities that will pull you off course. Let's purpose to understand what God has called us to do and keep our eyes on the unique path He has laid out for us.

I can't run your race. You can't run mine. But let's both commit to run with endurance and focus on the races set before us.

Mysterious Saying #4

Does Jesus want you to "hate" your parents, spouse, siblings, and children?

*H*ave you ever heard of the Donut Man? The Donut Man was a character at the center of a series of Christian music videos and audio recordings back in the 90s. My wife and I raised three daughters, and when our girls were little, the Donut Man videos and cassettes (Yes, cassettes! You have to be of a certain age to remember those.) were a fun and entertaining way to teach kids Scripture and scriptural principles.

For reasons that will immediately become obvious, one of our favorite Donut Man songs was based on the commandment "Honor your father and your mother." The song was "O-B-E-Y." And the chorus said, "O-B-E-Y, obey your mom and dad. O-B-E-Y, it makes them very glad." And it did. Parents will take all the help they can get, which puts me in remembrance of some hard-won wisdom I share with parents nowadays when I'm asked:

Three Rules for Parents

Rule 1. Never lose a test of wills with a three-year-old.

Rule 2. If at all possible, avoid getting into a test of wills with a three-year-old.

Rule 3. If you fail at Rule 2, see Rule 1.

Back when our crew was little, any time we ran into resistance or foot-dragging, we'd just start humming the tune to that song.

The commandment to honor your father and mother is one of the few of the original ten that gets an endorsement from Paul in the New Testament.

In Ephesians 6:2, Paul quotes it and points out that it's the only commandment that comes packaged with a promise.

That feels like a very strong endorsement for the whole "honor your parents thing" right? Which brings us to this particular "Mysterious Saying" of Jesus. In Luke 14, smack in the middle of a longer passage about counting the cost of following Him as a disciple, Jesus drops this bomb:

"If anyone comes to me and does not hate his own father and mother and wife and children and brothers and sisters, yes, and even his own life, he cannot be my disciple." (v. 26 ESV)

What are we going to do with that? I mean ... **hate** is a very strong word. Maybe something is being lost in translation here. Let's take a look at the Greek word underlying the English word "hate." The Greek word is *miseo*. It's a verb that means: "to hate, to pursue with hatred, or to detest." Oh well, it was worth a try.

There is a satisfying solution to this puzzle, though.

As is often the case, understanding a little history helps. And the answer here also lies in understanding that Jesus knew something that none of His listeners knew at that moment: His death was coming. And His death would be followed by His resurrection, His ascension to the throne, and His sending of the Holy Spirit to indwell a new kind of human being on the earth. A born-again human. One literally filled with the Spirit of God Himself. And that this would be made possible by a New Covenant that represents very good news, indeed. And, by God's plan, design, and command, the proclamation of that good news would be to the Jewish people first.

You may be familiar with Paul's words along these lines. Romans 1:16 says: "For I am not ashamed of the gospel, for it is the power of God for salvation to everyone who believes, to the Jew first and also to the Greek. [Gentile]" (ESV, addition mine)

Jesus wanted Jewish people to be the first to hear about the new and better covenant based on better promises that He was about to make possible. It's why Jesus' final instructions to His disciples in Acts 1:8 were heavy on geography:

> *"But you will receive power when the Holy Spirit has come upon you, and you will be my witnesses **in Jerusalem and in all Judea and Samaria, and to the end of the earth.**"* (ESV, emphasis added)

And indeed, the remaining eleven disciples did just that. They began their proclamations and declarations of the gospel in Jerusalem (3000 were saved on the first day!) and then fanned out from there, ultimately going wherever there were Jewish communities anywhere in the known world. And whenever they delivered that good news, Jewish hearts responded.

Jesus knew all of this well in advance. But He knew something else as well. When that day came, embracing that "good news" message and becoming a Jesus follower would likely cost Jewish hearers everything.

Those who said "yes" to Jesus would be disowned by their families. Lose their inheritances. Lose jobs, houses, and friends, too. If you want a good picture of what this was like, think about what it means to become a Jesus-follower today if you've grown up in a strict Islamic community. In many parts of the world, saying "yes" to the gospel of Jesus Christ means, at best, having your entire family say, "You're dead to us."

And often the consequences are far worse than simply becoming an outcast in your own family.

Two chapters earlier in Luke, Jesus had sounded a similar warning about what was coming. In Luke 12:51–53, Jesus says:

> *"Do you think that I have come to give peace on earth? No, I tell you, but rather division. For from now on in one house there will be five divided, three against two and two against three. They will be divided, father against son and son against father, mother against daughter and daughter against mother, mother-in-law against her daughter-in-law and daughter-in-law against mother-in-law."* (ESV)

Yes, Jesus knew this was coming. So in the spirit of "truth in advertising," He warned everyone who intended to follow Him that a time would come where they would likely have to choose between Him and family acceptance.

THAT, dear friend, is what Jesus was saying when He declared that anyone who followed Him would need to, comparatively, "hate" his or her own family. Indeed, many who said yes to the gospel likely heard crying family members shout, "Why are you doing this?! Why do you hate us?!"

Jesus had this same sobering reality in mind in the opening verses of John 16:

> *"I have said all these things to you to keep you from falling away. They will put you out of the synagogues. Indeed, the hour is coming when whoever kills you will think he is offering service to God. And they will do these things because they have not known the Father, nor me. But I have said these things to you, that when their hour comes you may remember that I told them to you."* (John 16:1–4 ESV)

Just a few verses earlier, Jesus had said,

"If the world hates you, know that it has
hated me before it hated you. If you were of
the world, the world would love you as its
own; but because you are not of the world,
but I chose you out of the world, therefore the
world hates you. Remember the word that
I said to you: 'A servant is not greater than
his master.' If they persecuted me, they will
also persecute you." (John 15:18–20 ESV)

So, another mystery is solved. For the people listening to Jesus' words, a day was coming where they'd likely have to choose between Him and family. And if you're ever faced with that dilemma, HE is always the right choice.

Now let's examine what practical help and inspiration we can take away from this new understanding.

First, we can say that the Donut Man was right. You *should* honor your father and mother in every way you can ... UNLESS they demand that you reject Jesus and His extraordinary offer of forgiveness, wholeness, and eternal life. If your family insists on standing between you and saying "Yes" to Jesus, well, your love for Him should make your affection for your family look like "hate" in comparison.

Second, we should take note that even though you may not be living in first-century Judea or modern-day Iran, saying "Yes" to Jesus is still likely to cost you something. It will certainly cost you your pride. We can only come to the cross empty-handed.

It might cost you friends. It has for a lot of us.

It could very well cost you prestige or social status. The hard truth of Jesus' warnings is that His followers are rarely invited to sit at the "cool kids table" in the school lunchroom of the dominant culture. We can and should admire the fact that Jesus was a starkly honest salesman. Here's His sales pitch, in Big Dave's Unauthorized Paraphrase Version:

"They hated me. Follow me and they'll hate you, too. So how about it? Up for an adventure? It will be the adventure of the ages!"

Mysterious Saying #5

Did Jesus really say He was leaving
the Old Testament law in place?

*H*ow do you please God? What does He expect? Should you just try your best to obey the Ten Commandments and the rest of the Law? Or should you simply love everyone and be led by the Spirit of God? You can be excused if you're confused about that. Because the letters of Paul seem to give one answer, and the Scripture we're going to examine today—a direct statement from Jesus—on the surface, seems to say the opposite. I'm talking about Matthew 5:17–18. There, Jesus said:

*"Do not think that I have come to abolish the Law or the Prophets; I have not come to abolish them **but to fulfill them.** For truly, I say to you, until heaven and earth pass away, not an iota, not a dot, will pass from the Law until all is accomplished."* (ESV, emphasis added)

Many well-meaning believers have taken Jesus' statement that He did not come to abolish the Law to mean that He was leaving the Old Covenant regulations in place—if not all of them, at least a large chunk of them.

We're about to see that that's just not the case.

The New Testament books of Galatians and Hebrews make it clear that this cannot possibly be what He meant. And we've already seen in a couple of instances that when Jesus and Paul don't appear on the surface to be on the same page, it's because we've failed to grasp that Jesus had a prophetic mission to the nation of Israel that preceded His priestly and kingly assignment to the whole world. Many of the "red letter" passages in our Bibles reveal Jesus operating as a prophet to a specific generation of Jewish people. (As an exercise, do an online Bible search of the books of Matthew and Luke for the term "this generation." When Jesus looked a crowd in the face and said "this generation" ... guess what? ... He meant the generation of the people who were hearing His words at that moment.)

In this particular case, understanding what Jesus meant hinges on understanding the meaning of the word "fulfill" in His statement. Please note, He said He did not come to abolish the Law but to FULFILL it.

His true meaning comes sharply into focus when you realize the Old Covenant viewed the Law and its requirements as an obligation to be "paid" to God. And that failing to meet that obligation—failing to keep the Law—resulted in a "debt" to God. Paul had this sense of debt or obligation in mind when he wrote in Colossians 2:13–14:

*And you, who were dead in your trespasses and
the uncircumcision of your flesh, God made
alive together with him [Jesus], having forgiven
us all our trespasses, by canceling the record
of **DEBT** that stood against us with its legal
demands. This he set aside, nailing it to the
cross.* (ESV, addition and emphasis added)

You see here the sense of sin being a "debt" to God.
Simply "abolishing" the Law would have left the
debt unpaid—the obligation unmet. But Jesus' glorious answer when He was asked if He came to abolish
the Law was, "No. I came to fulfill it." In other words,
"I have come to completely fulfill, once and for all, the
obligation of the Law!"

He came to satisfy my debt to the Law. Your debt, too.

He came to "fulfill" our obligation to it. That's
something none of us had the capital to do ourselves.
It's just too big and we're just too flawed.

We could not satisfy our debt to the perfect, immutable law of God. And God, in His righteousness, could not simply sweep that debt away with a wave of His hand. No, the obligation to the Law had to be satisfied. Or put another way ... Fulfilled!

So Jesus came and did that ... for you and for me.

We see this confirmed in some of the Savior's final words from the cross. His very last words were basically a prayer. A prayer of childlike faith. He said, "Father, into your hands I entrust My spirit" just before He took his final breath. (Luke 23:46 HCSB) But only moments earlier, the witnesses gathered around the dying Savior heard Him shout something else, a single word that was basically, oddly enough, a Greek accounting term: *"Tetelestai!"*

We find it in John 19:30: "When Jesus had received the sour wine, he said, 'It is finished,' and he bowed his head and gave up his spirit" (ESV).

Underneath that simple phrase, "It is finished," is the Greek word *tetelestai*. Our English Bibles translate that term in a way that drains it of power and conceals the legal and financial connotations it clearly carried for hearers of Jesus' day. The best most translators can come up with is the plain-vanilla phrase, "It is finished." Others say, "It is completed" or "It is accomplished." None of these translations are anywhere near adequate to convey that word's extraordinary meaning and implications.

Tetelestai doesn't just mean that a thing has concluded.

It does not simply indicate that the plus-sized lady with the Viking horns has sung, the curtain has come down, and the show is over. That Porky Pig has stammered out, "That's All Folks!" To declare a thing *tetelestai* is to decree that ALL has been accomplished, everything formerly lacking has now been supplied. The wound has been healed. The obligation has been met. The debt has been completely satisfied!

Okay, now brace yourself for some grammar talk. Remember grammar? It's okay, you'll survive this. *Tetelestai* is a verb— an action word. And verbs have tenses. And the tense of the verb Jesus used is *perfect passive indicative tense*. That's right, you heard me. "Perfect passive indicative" means that an action has been completed, but that the results of that action will continue with full effect going forward. In other words, what Jesus accomplished on the cross was total and complete satisfaction of a debt, and it would continue to be paid in full for all time.

Jesus' *"Tetelestai!"* declared an end to man's religious striving to build a ladder to heaven. God Himself had come down and done what no fallen man could do: satisfy mankind's staggering legal and spiritual obligation to divine justice.

That's why it was one of Jesus' final declarations from the cross. He shouted "Paid in full! The obligation has been fully met!"

THAT resolves the apparent, superficial conflict between Paul and Jesus. Jesus said He'd come to

FULFILL our obligation to the Law. Paul said, "That's exactly what He did!"

So, what are our takeaways here?

Well, maybe a story from my college years will help you here. Have you ever loaned money to a friend in a desperate situation? I did. I had a friend, a guy very dear to me, and I knew this friend was in a financial jam. He asked for a loan. I had the money in my savings account, so I loaned it to him. He, of course, promised to repay me when the crisis was over.

The problem was the crisis didn't end. It just evolved into a worse pickle. So, my friend couldn't repay it in a timely way. I knew he was going through a hard time. I understood. And I still loved him and loved hanging out with him. I was rooting for him.

Nevertheless, you know what happened. My friend started avoiding me like I had the Ebola virus. He ghosted me ... the one person who'd gone out of his way to help him. It's a sad but very common phenomenon. Even among the closest of friends, embarrassment and shame keep debtor and lender apart as long as the obligation remains "unfulfilled."

This same dynamic was in place for thousands of years in mankind's relationship to God. Adam and Eve's sin put them (and us) in deep debt to God's eternal, immutable bank of justice. And as with my college friend who borrowed money, we instinctively avoid Him, even though He loves us and wants the best for us. (Adam and Eve's immediate impulse after incurring their sin-debt was to hide from God.)

Maybe you've been avoiding Him for the same reason.

Here's what you need to know.

Your heavenly Father sent Jesus to pay your debt in full. Through His sacrifice, the demands of holy justice woven into the fabric of the universe at the moment of creation were fully satisfied. You can now rejoice in the glorious truth that you can come to Him with no sense of obligation, indebtedness, or shame.

God came looking for Adam and Eve. He wants relationship with us.

There's an old saying about what Jesus did to make that relationship possible:

> I owed a debt I could not pay.
> He paid a debt He did not owe.

As a result, you can come to your heavenly Father with confidence and faith. Why? Because you know your debt to God has been fully paid. Jesus picked up the check.

He did not come and set aside Law. He fulfilled it. On your behalf and mine. That means we're debt free. We're not obligated to it any longer.

Mysterious Saying #6

Did something surprise Jesus while on the cross?

*D*id something take Jesus, the Son of God, by surprise? Was He confused, startled, and disoriented? A certain scripture in Mark seems to suggest this. Let's take a look at it and explore the question. Here's Mark 15:34 (NIV):

> *And at three in the afternoon Jesus cried out in a loud voice, "Eloi, Eloi, lama sabachthani?" ("My God, my God, why have you forsaken me?" in Aramaic)*

To better understand why Jesus said these words, I need to take you to the scene.

Jesus' closest friends have all run away. They've scurried home, deadbolted the doors, and drawn the curtains. A trusted associate has betrayed Jesus to His bitter, murderous enemies and, to add insult to injury, one of His two closest friends has denied he even knows Him. The darkest day any human has ever known has only gotten darker with each passing minute.

The huge crowds that followed him everywhere seeking help and favors are now nowhere to be seen. Only a few days ago they had greeted His arrival with singing, dancing, and palm-branch waving. Now they all seem to have remembered urgent business to which they must attend.

Now that He's hanging on a cross, the only ones still around are His enemies. Oh, and a handful of skeptics who hurl taunts and insults at Him from a safe distance. Only now that He is securely nailed in place have they found the courage to mock Him openly.

Both darkness and silence wrap the hillside like a thick blanket. Then the quiet is torn in two by a shout ... more of a wail actually, in Aramaic: "Eli! Eli! Lama sabachthani!" "My God, my God, why have you forsaken me?"

In the centuries since that heart-rending cry rang out across the rocky hills outside Jerusalem's walls, countless readers of the Bible have wondered about it. It's a puzzle because Jesus seems to express ... surprise or bewilderment. This doesn't seem right to us because one thing Jesus NEVER once showed in His previous thirty-three years on earth was confusion. Nothing blindsided Him. He always knew what God was doing and what people were thinking.

So what's the deal here? Was Jesus—God in human flesh—actually caught by surprise as He hung on the cross? The short answer is "no."

Despite the appearance, Jesus' cry is NOT an expression of surprise.

Our Savior is not bewildered here. No, He is simply doing what He had always done in moments of stress or spiritual warfare. He is quoting Scripture.

What Scripture? Psalm 22:1 (NASB):

> *My God, my God, why have You*
> *forsaken me? Far from my help are*
> *the words of my groaning.*

But why? Why would Jesus quote THIS Scripture at THIS moment? The answer comes into focus if we zoom out a bit and look at more of that same psalm. Later on, we find these words:

> *I am poured out like water, and*
> *all my bones are out of joint.*
>
> *My heart has turned to wax; it*
> *has melted within me.*

My mouth is dried up like a potsherd,
and my tongue sticks to the roof of my
mouth; you lay me in the dust of death.

Dogs surround me, a pack of villains encircles
me; they pierce my hands and my feet.

All my bones are on display; people
stare and gloat over me.

They divide my clothes among them
and cast lots for my garment.
(Psalm 22:14–18 NIV)

Do you see it? This psalm almost seems to have been written by an eyewitness to the crucifixion. The psalmist David had prophetically looked down through the centuries and was granted a look at his descendant on the cross for a brief, horrifying moment. Of course, Jesus knew the Old Testament scriptures at a depth hard for us to imagine.

Is it any wonder Jesus had this particular psalm on His mind as He hung on the cross?

He was experiencing it verse by terrible verse.

Yes, Jesus is a man of the Scriptures. Which is why an amazing percentage of the red-letter words in our Bibles are direct references to Old Testament passages. It seems Jesus defined His life, His mission, and His message purely and wholly in the light of the Scriptures. It seems that every circumstance and every challenge brought a verse to Jesus' mind and mouth. When confronted by the devil, Jesus quoted the Bible. He cited it to answer His disciples' endless questions. He quoted it to refute and confound the Sadducees, Pharisees, and Sanhedrin.

But now ... hanging alone between heaven and earth, He has no one to quote it to but Himself.

Friend, never has a person been so alone as Jesus of Nazareth was on the day He was crucified. As the accumulated sin and depravity of an entire race fell upon one Man, a pure and holy Father was forced to withdraw His life-giving, comforting presence from His only begotten Son. As Jesus felt His Father pull away—as He learned for the first time in His eternal existence what it meant to be separated from God the Father—a scripture came to mind.

That's the takeaway for you and me today!

Jesus knew something that you and I need to learn:

In dark moments, we must cling to the words of God. And in the darkest moment any person has ever endured, His tortured soul reached out, grasping for orienting comfort. So, He quoted a messianic prophecy that pointed to the very moment He was experiencing. He quotes it to remind Himself who He is, what He is doing, and why it must be done. The work He has begun must be finished.

So ... was Jesus caught by surprise by something as He hung on the cross?

The answer is no. Jesus was not expressing surprise. He, as always, was giving voice to the Bible. If Jesus needed to know and speak scripture, surely you and I do, too.

Mysterious Saying #7

Did Jesus really call Satan
"The God of this World"?

There's a funny line in the opening scene of the Coen Brothers movie, "O, Brother, Where Art Thou." If you've seen it, (and who hasn't?!) you know it's set in the deep south in the 1930s; and three convicts are shackled together and trying to escape a chain-gang work crew. Everett, the instigator played by George Clooney, has provided a plan. But Pete, played by John Turturro, isn't convinced. So he protests, "Wait a minute. Who elected you leader of this outfit?"

I'll whip that line out every so often in a group when one assertive person is trying to decide the choice of restaurant.

That's a question we can ask concerning this fallen, broken world. "Who's running the show?" is an important question. "Who's in charge?"

We're taught from childhood that God, who made this world, is running it. But then when you look around and see all the heartache, misery, oppression, tragedy, and pain ... questions arise. Especially when you know in your knower that God is good. And kind. And He is.

Which brings us to a startling proclamation from the mouth of Jesus Himself.

In John 14, Jesus is beginning a long, super-important conversation with His inner circle. It's important because He knows, as we now know, that in just a few hours He's going to be arrested, tried, tortured, and crucified.

In the previous chapter (13), we see Jesus washing the disciples' feet and eating his final meal with them. Then chapters 14, 15, and 16 record his final instructions to them. Chapter 17 records his final prayer for them.

So what does Jesus say in John 14:30–31 (ESV) that is so shocking? Let's read it:

> *"I will no longer talk much with you, for the ruler of this world is coming. He has no claim on me, but I do as the Father has commanded me, so that the world may know that I love the Father. Rise, let us go from here."*

It is universally understood that Jesus is referring to Satan here ... who He calls "the ruler of this world." Wait ... what? Really? Let's check some other translations to make sure we're reading that right.

The New American Standard? *"the ruler of the world."*

New King James? *"the ruler of this world."*

The NIV? *"The PRINCE of this world."*

Pretty much every major translation has Jesus calling Satan either "the ruler of the world," "the ruler of THIS world," or the "PRINCE of this world." The Passion Translation renders it: "the ruler of this dark world."

So, what is Jesus revealing with this statement?

Is Satan running the show here? Or least was he back then? And if so, "Who elected him leader of this outfit?"

Okay, friend. I've got answers for you. To get them, we'll take a peek under the hood and look at the Greek words Jesus used in that statement. And we'll also take a little side trip back to Genesis for some key insight. Stay with me here because there is VERY good news waiting for you at the end of this little journey.

Now remember, Jesus said, "'the ruler of this world' is coming for me." The Greek word *archon* Jesus used here is translated "ruler" or "prince." And underneath the word "world" is the Greek word *kosmos*. So, Jesus called the devil, "the *archon* of this *kosmos*." Got it?

Let's work backward on those two words. Obviously, *kosmos* looks a lot like our word cosmos, and with good reason. It's where we get it. In English, cosmos refers to the universe. So is Jesus calling Satan the ruler of the universe? No way.

In biblical Greek, *kosmos* has a wide variety of meanings. It can mean the world, as in "the planet earth;" or the sky and the visible stars; or "an ordered system or organizational hierarchy." When used to refer to an ordered system, it suggests the opposite of chaos. For example, in the modern world, we have an ordered financial-economic system, right? That global system of finance is a type of *kosmos*.

Yes, *kosmos* can take on different meanings, just as our word "land" does. Think about it. "Land" can refer to all the non-water parts of the planet—as in "dry land." It can refer to a nation or a country—as in, "I come from a land down under!" and "She's the fairest maiden in the land." Or land can refer to a plot of dirt. "Get off of my land!" One English word has multiple meanings. We learn to determine which of those meanings is intended by picking up on context clues. The same is true for Greek words like *kosmos*.

So, which meaning of the word *kosmos* did Jesus intend when He called Satan "the archon of this *kosmos?*" We'll get to that in a moment. First, let's look at that other key word *archon*.

So what's an **archon**?

Well, in the governmental systems (there's that word "system" again) of the Greek and Roman empires, an *archon* was an administrator or ruler put in charge of a city or province by the emperor. Both ancient empires were divided up into provinces and territories, and the emperor would designate a governor or administrator called an *archon* over each one. Sometimes an archon was one of the sons of the emperor, so ... a prince. The archon had legal, delegated authority. He ran the place because the emperor had decreed it legally to be so.

Now let's return to Jesus' stunning description of Satan as "the *archon* of this *kosmos*." Let's assume for a moment that Jesus was saying that Satan was the legal ruler of this world or this world's systems. Because that seems to be what He's saying.

If that's the case, it would solve another mystery or puzzle from the Gospels. Namely, something puzzling that was said when Jesus was in the wilderness for 40 days being tempted by Satan. As you may recall, the first temptation Jesus—who hadn't eaten anything in weeks—faced was to turn stones into bread. When that failed, God's mortal enemy brought forward what he surely thought was an even more tempting offer. In case you're not familiar with that, let's take a quick look at it:

> *And he [Satan] led Him up and showed Him* **all the kingdoms of the world** *in a moment of time. And the devil said to Him, "I will give You all this domain and its glory,* **for it has been handed over to me, and I give it to whomever I want.** *Therefore, if You worship*

before me, it shall all be Yours." Jesus replied to him, "It is written: 'You shall worship the Lord your God and serve Him only.'" (Luke 4:5–8 NASB, additions mine, emphasis added)

Keep in mind here that the only way this offer could be a legitimate temptation for Jesus is if the devil really could deliver what he offered. Otherwise, Jesus would have just laughed it off.

I'm not in any way tempted to buy the Brooklyn Bridge from you for a dollar when I know you don't own the Brooklyn Bridge.

No, the evidence and logic are pretty inescapable here. In some sense, somewhere along the line, Satan had become the legal ruler of this world or its systems. Earth's *archon*. But when? How?

The answer lies in the opening chapters of Genesis. There we see God ... the Creator-Emperor of the universe ... of all the universes ... delegating legal authority over this planet to a couple of humans and their descendants. (See: Genesis 1:26–28 and 2:15)

Here's an overview of what those opening chapters of Genesis describe. God creates a beautifully perfect but wild and untamed world. He cultivates a little piece of it, creating a garden. Then He places them in it and says, in essence, "Be fruitful, multiply, take dominion over nature because I've delegated authority over this place to you and your descendants. I legally declare you (Adam and Eve and your descendants) the *archons* of the earth."

Of course, we know that things went horribly wrong not too long after. And although the details of how this happened are fuzzy, we have to conclude that Adam and Eve's bow to the Serpent and to his temptation in the garden had the effect of transferring the legal *archon*-ship of planet earth from them to him. Which is why we have no less authority than Jesus referring to Satan as "the ruler of this world."

Which brings us to another question. Is that still the case?

Does the devil still have some small measure of legal control over this brilliant blue marble? Well, here is where the news gets really good. I mean jump-up-and-run-around-the-room good.

Jesus made His "ruler of this world is coming" statement with the cross right in front of Him. Well, when the cross was right *behind* Him. Just a few weeks after His resurrection and just before He ascended into the heaven, Jesus said THIS to those same disciples:

> And Jesus came and said to them, **"All authority in heaven and on earth has been given to me.** Go therefore and make disciples of all nations, baptizing them in the name of the Father and of the Son and of the Holy Spirit, teaching them to observe all that I have commanded you."
> (Matthew 28:18–20a ESV, emphasis added)

Do you get the impression that something had changed in those weeks? That through the cross, something in the legal order of the universe had been restored to its original setting, perhaps? Because it sounds like Jesus is saying the earth has a new *archon*. It took millennia to bring about, but a new "Adam" was once again in charge.

And just like God had made Adam and Eve the original *archons* of the planet and then commissioned them to be fruitful, multiply, and subdue it ... here, the new, restored *archon* is saying pretty much the same thing to His brothers and sisters. Do you see it? Jesus basically told his disciples to fan out across the planet and "be fruitful and multiply" by making disciples.

How did that transfer of legal authority happen?

Well, fortunately, the Apostle Paul offers some insight into that question.

In Colossians 2, Paul is describing all the amazing things Jesus accomplished for us through the cross. Then in verse 15 we read: "He disarmed the rulers and authorities and put them to open shame, by triumphing over them in Him." (ESV)

But you get a better sense of what Paul is describing here in The Passion Translation:

> *Then Jesus made a public spectacle of all the*
> *powers and principalities of darkness, stripping*
> *away from them every weapon and all their*
> *spiritual authority and power to accuse us.*
> *And by the power of the cross, Jesus led them*
> *around as prisoners in a procession of triumph.*
> *He was not their prisoner; they were his!*

Yes! What the first Adam had legally forfeited to God's enemy in the fall ... the Last Adam restored in His death and resurrection!

So let's circle back to the original mystery we're exploring here. Yes, Jesus knew precisely what He was talking about when, prior to the cross, He called the devil the *archon* of this *kosmos* ... the ruler of this world and its worldly systems of order. But a key part of His victory through the cross involved stripping the *archon* of His legal authority and standing.

Jesus was equally correct when, on the edge of ascending to take His seat on the throne at God's right hand, He said, "ALL authority ... in both heaven and on earth ... have been given to me." That's very good news.

So let's explore some takeaways for you and me.

The devil didn't disappear or cease to exist when Jesus emerged from the tomb two thousand years ago. But something very significant *had* changed. The day before, Satan had operated with some level of legal authority on this planet. The authority of an *archon* he had swindled and conned away from the rightful office holders, Adam and Eve (and their future offspring).

From the day of Jesus' victory forward, the devil was reduced to the status of an outlaw. A trespasser. A squatter living on territory where he has no legal claim. The *archon*-ship of planet earth had been restored to a human once again. And not just to Him, but to every person "in Him." According to Ephesians 2:5–6, every person who is "in Christ" has been raised up with Christ and is seated with Him in heavenly places.

The old evil *archon* has been deposed. Enjoy taking your place in the glorious administration of earth's rightful reigning *archon* in this era and the ages to come. That's our Savior. Our elder brother, Jesus.

That means you don't need to fear the devil. There's no need to dread him. Jesus stripped and disarmed him. Made a public spectacle of him and his underlings. The fact is his only remaining weapon is deception. All he can do is get you to believe a lie. And you have God's Word and His Spirit to lead you into all truth.

Mysteries Solved

Well, if you've stuck with me through this journey into the words and actions of our wonderful Savior, then you now have a deeper appreciation for how amazing He truly is. And you're likely coming away with more than just insights into some passages that have puzzled Bible readers for centuries. You should also have some tools and a grid to help you better understand everything else Jesus did and said in the Gospels! For example:

You now know that historical and cultural context is often a key to explaining something that seems odd to you and me today.

Even more important in the Gospels is the understanding that for much of Jesus' ministry, He was functioning as a prophet to a specific, special generation of Jewish people. If you want a quick eye-opening exercise, go to an online Bible site and search the books of Matthew and Luke for the phrase "this generation." Jesus said "this generation" over and over again ... and for a reason. He was speaking a momentously important prophetic word to the people who were actually hearing His words at that moment. This understanding also snaps many of Jesus' difficult-to-understand parables into focus. Yes, there is meaning in those words for you and me today, but their initial, primary meaning was for those who actually heard them. And it's vital to grasp that meaning before we start trying to apply them to ourselves.

Finally, you've learned that even when to our modern ears and sensibilities Jesus seems harsh or hard ... He's actually being redemptive. He was ever and always passionate about the mission a loving heavenly Father had sent Him to accomplish.

He explained that mission to a man named Nicodemus one evening. He explained His entire purpose in two sentences ... in John 3:16–17 (ESV). There Jesus says:

> *"For God so loved the world that he gave his only Son, that whoever believes in him should not perish but have eternal life. For God did not send his Son into the world to condemn the world, but in order that the world might be saved through him."*

Everything Jesus did and said had that mission in mind. Which means He had YOU and me in mind ... all the way to and through the cross. Trust Him. Trust the One who sent Him.

About the Author

David A. Holland is a writer, speaker, teacher, husband, father, and grandfather—carrying a call to help God's people better comprehend His extraordinary goodness and extravagant grace.

His writing on faith, life, and culture—along with a wide array of other resources—is accessible at **DavidAHolland.com**.

𝕏 @DavidHolland

◎ @DavidAHolland

f /DavidAHolland.Inspires

▶ @DavidAHolland

www.ingramcontent.com/pod-product-compliance
Lightning Source LLC
Chambersburg PA
CBHW051631120626
46551CB00014B/2035